Activity Book

Calling all Moshling hunters! Greetings, Buster Bumblechops, super Moshling expert, here. Now, although I am fangtastic at catching these tricky little critters, I might just need your help today, because a few of them are proving more than a bit difficult to catch. Keep your eyes peeled (not literally!) in the pages of this book for CocoLoco, Tiamo, Suey and Shelly, they're teeny-weeny masters of hide-and-seek. Happy hunting!

Can you also prick your paw on this Catacactus?

Myrtle Turtle's Treasure Hunt

Myrtle the Diving Turtle is world-renowned for her treasure hunting ability but prefers to stay in the water. Help her find this treasure on land by grabbing your compass and seeing if you can match her TURTLEy tremendous treasure seeking skills. Follow the clues carefully and who knows what you might find? (Hint: Tricky to earn, easy to spend! Pieces of eight!)

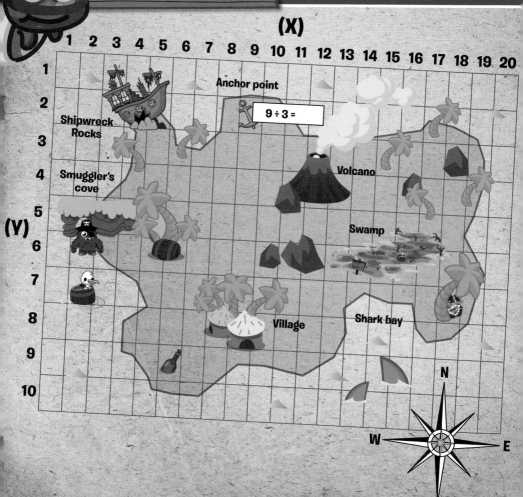

(X)

1 2 3 4 5 6 7 8 9 10 11 12 13 14 15 16 17 18 19 20

(Y)

1 2 3 4 5 6 7 8 9 10

Shipwreck Rocks

Anchor point

$9 \div 3 =$

Smuggler's cove

Volcano

Swamp

Village

Shark bay

N

W E

S

Find the message in the bottle to start your quest.

1 Go north three squares, then west two squares.

2 Cap'n Buck has your next clue.
Go to where he sends you . . .

> Head towards something that will stop a ship drifting out to sea.

3 The answer to the puzzle you find there will give you a number – move that many squares south.

4 Now turn to the east and move six squares.

5 Answer this question for your next move:
How many buckets are there on Bleurgh Beach?

Move this number of squares north.

6 Nearly there! Take sixty-nine away from Cali's number and move this number of squares east.

#072

7 Finally, do this sum, 10 + 6 – 12, and then move the number of squares in the answer south, to find the treasure.

Lefty's Look-out

In a sword fight with a seagull, shipmate Lefty lost a tentacle that left him unable to balance on the deck of the *Cloudy Cloth Clipper*. Now he's forever destined to spend his seafaring days up in the crow's nest, calling out "Land ho!" Take over the watch to give this ol' sea dog a break.

1. TINACAP UKBC

2. ASELSLEH

3. LĄCI

Call

4. YLOJL OGRER

5. MUBELF

6. TUCKEB DNA PASED

4

Shipshape!

A. Don't be afraid, Roger thinks it's jolly!

B. Drop it to stop the ship.

C. Every monster needs these sparkly gems to live in Monstro City.

D. Even earmuffs won't block out the ear-splitting ditties of this whistling sea critter.

E. Cap'n Buck just wouldn't be a salty sea dog without this.

F. An extra eye that helps you see near and far at the same time.

Gail Whale's Enormous Word Search

Blasting blow-holes! Like her energetic enormous self, Gail Whale doesn't do anything by half. She's been scouring the seas and around Monstro City looking for new things to discover. Search this monster word grid to see what she's seen and where she's been. (Now there's a tongue twister if I ever heard one!).

S	E	L	T	R	V	M	Z	X	L	E	F	T	Y
E	Q	N	R	E	G	O	R	Y	L	L	O	J	N
L	B	U	B	B	L	E	B	A	T	H	B	A	Y
S	E	V	E	N	T	Y	S	E	A	S	Q	X	C
I	U	P	O	T	I	O	N	O	C	E	A	N	L
E	M	P	Z	X	K	Q	Z	D	R	N	O	R	O
U	R	A	U	F	I	U	O	J	U	T	N	K	U
Q	V	T	X	M	R	O	J	M	C	H	Z	F	D
I	F	C	K	V	W	Q	K	O	A	W	P	R	Y
T	B	H	O	Y	Q	Z	W	P	L	F	M	S	C
N	Z	F	L	H	F	W	K	P	I	J	K	H	L
A	J	L	R	V	I	N	M	Y	U	K	Q	J	O
K	O	D	N	A	L	S	I	T	F	I	G	Z	T
J	R	B	L	E	U	R	G	H	B	E	A	C	H

POTION OCEAN
BUBBLEBATH BAY
BLEURGH BEACH
GIFT ISLAND
PATCH
LEFTY
OCTO
MYRTLE
ANTIQUE ISLE
CLOUDY CLOTH
JOLLY ROGER
JOLLYWOOD
CALI
TIKI
SEVENTY SEAS

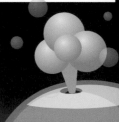

Land Ahoy!

Don't get your flippers in a twist! You may be seeing double, but just wash the salty seawater out of your eyes (however many you have!), and you can find out what Gail Whale's latest discovery is.

Grab a pen and cross out the letters that appear more than once in the grid below. Rearrange the remaining letters to reveal the name of the place Gail has found!

Q	T	Z	Y	T	H	W	X	O	H
O	E	D	V	F	T	U	B	F	E
Y	J	W	P	K	V	W	Y	J	G
P	C	F	H	A	Z	P	V	N	K
X	O	H	L	B	E	O	J	X	H
P	K	Y	X	E	J	O	M	W	Z
B	P	E	T	Q	H	Q	G	T	V
G	V	K	W	F	I	Z	T	G	H
Z	S	B	G	V	F	J	Q	B	Y
E	K	O	X	Y	H	W	K	F	J

_ _ _ _ I _   _ S _ _ _ _ _

Cap'n Buck's
Message in a Bottle

That salty ol' sea dog, Cap'n Buck is in a spot of bother. As all pirates know, the best thing to do in a sticky situation is to send out a message in a bottle, and then, arrrr, wait . . . well, it's either that or you might as well just walk the plank!

Crack the piratey code to find out what the Cap'n's message was. There might be some pieces of eight in it for ye!

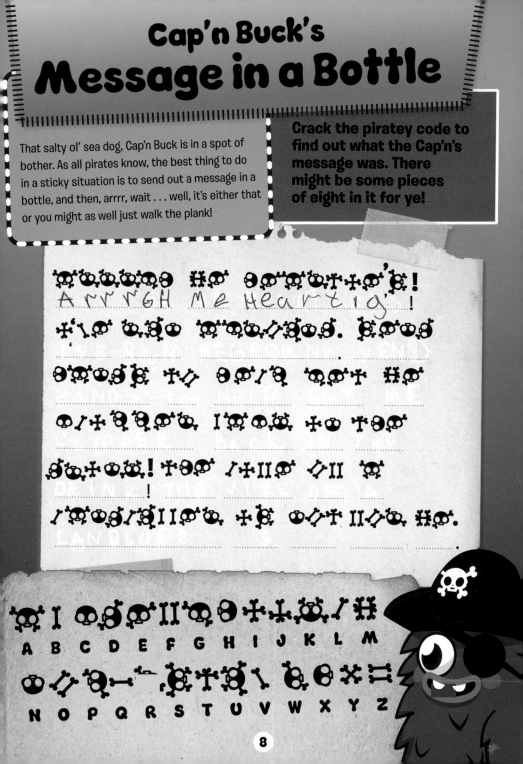

8

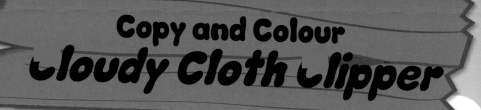

Copy and Colour
Cloudy Cloth Clipper

Shiver me timbers! I was so busy jabbering with me hearties, that I didna notice that pesky ol' Glumpy fella sneak on board and mess up me trusty ol' ship. Help me get the *Cloudy Cloth* all shipshape again. All hands on deck! Arrrrr!

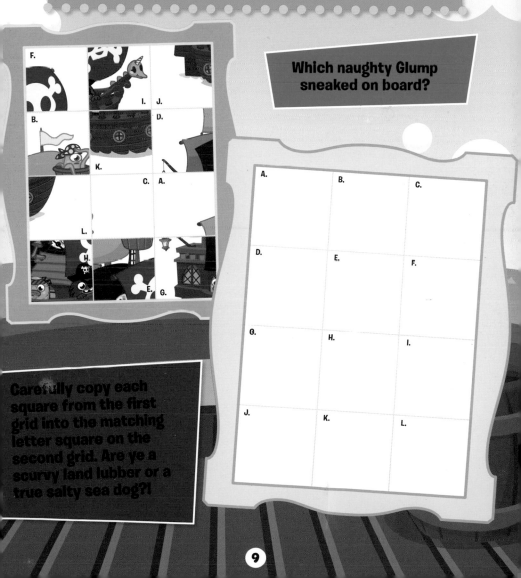

Which naughty Glump sneaked on board?

Carefully copy each square from the first grid into the matching letter square on the second grid. Are ye a scurvy land lubber or a true salty sea dog?!

9

Spot the
Mushi Difference

Every monster likes to take a little holiday from their busy life in the city, and where better to relax than on the beach? Bleurgh Beach is the happenin' hairy hangout for any monster in the know. Grab your swimsuit and shades and come and sizzle by the sea.

Check out who's getting sand between their hairy toes, and try and spot the ten differences between these two sunny scenes.

Patch's
Picture Puzzles

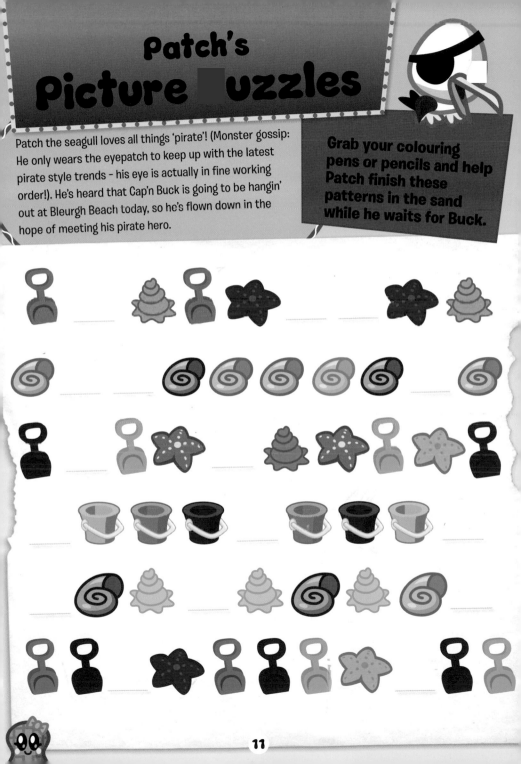

Patch the seagull loves all things 'pirate'! (Monster gossip: He only wears the eyepatch to keep up with the latest pirate style trends - his eye is actually in fine working order!). He's heard that Cap'n Buck is going to be hangin' out at Bleurgh Beach today, so he's flown down in the hope of meeting his pirate hero.

Grab your colouring pens or pencils and help Patch finish these patterns in the sand while he waits for Buck.

Potion Ocean
Mystery

Who knows how many weird and wonderful monsters lurk down in the murky depths of Potion Ocean? Not even Gail or Myrtle, with all their monstrous searching skills, have managed to uncover this Moshi mystery.

Clean the sand and furballs out of your brain, and take a guess yourself. Draw a picture of the creature that you think dwells there. Give it a fangtastic monstrous name!

Fumble's Fishy Fact or Fib Quiz

1 Acrobatic SeaStars hate to body surf. Fact or Fib?

2 Acrobatic SeaStars love to show off their death-defying acrobatic stunts. Fact or Fib?

3 Valley Mermaids hang out in the Sea Mall deep beneath Potion Ocean. Fact or Fib?

4 Batty Bubblefish are soft and fluffy. Fact or Fib?

5 Valley Mermaids' hearts flash whenever they sense romance. Fact or Fib?

6 Beau Squiddly spends all his time fishing. Fact or Fib?

7 Songful SeaHorses are excellent swimmers. Fact or Fib?

8 Billy Bob Baitman is great at catching fish. Fact or Fib?

9 The shifty, tentacled owner of Dodgy Dealz is called Sly Change. Fact or Fib?

10 Seen from above, Bleurgh Beach has six palm trees. Fact or Fib?

Where are the Birdies?

Fill in the number of times you can find each Moshling in the circles below.

3

4

2

3

Batty
Cap'n Buck!

Lift your eyepatch and take a peek at these two odd one out puzzles. One of the Batty Bubblefish isn't quite as batty as the others. And everthin' isn't shipshape with one of the ol' barnacley sea dogs.

Ahoy there me hearties! Did you know that your very own intrepid sea explorer and top hairy pirate, Captain Buck E. Barnacle, was orphaned by a terrible shipwreck and raised by a school of Batty Bubblefish? (That explains a lot, don't you think?!) I thought there was a strange resemblance between Blurp and the Cap'n!

You know the drill by now - if you get them correct there will be pieces of eight in it for you. If not . . . yes, you know what you have to do. WALK THE PLANK!

1.

2.

3.

4.

5.

6.

A.

B.

C.

D.

E.

F.

Answers

Title page:
Tiamo is hidden on p.4; Suey is hidden on p.7; Shelly is hidden on p.11; Cocoloco is hidden on p.15; and the Catacactus is hidden on p.10.

Pages 2-3
Myrtle Turtle's Treasure Hunt
The treasure is hidden on square 7Y,18X. It is a glittering pile of Rox.

Page 4
Lefty's Look-out
1. TINACAP UKBC - Captain Buck
2. ASE LSLEH - Seashell
3. LACI - Cali
4. YLOJL OGRER - Jolly Roger
5. MUBELF - Fumble
6. TUCKEB DNA PASED - Bucket and spade

Page 5
Shipshape!
A. Skull and crossbones.
B. Anchor.
C. A pile of Rox.
D. Stanley the Songful Seahorse.
E. Cap'n Buck's pirate hat.
F. A telescope.

Page 6
Gail Whale's Enormous Word Search

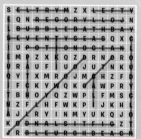

Page 7
Land Ahoy!
Gail Whale has discovered Music Island.

Page 8
Cap'n Buck's Message in a Bottle
Arrrgh me hearties! I've run aground. Send hands to help get me Clipper back in the drink! The life of a landlubber is not for me.

Page 9
Copy and Colour Cloudy Cloth Clipper

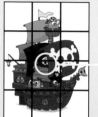

Pirate Pong sneaked on board.

Page 10
Spot the Moshi Difference

Page 11
Patch's Picture Puzzles

Page 13
Fumble's Fishy Fact or Fib Quiz
1 Fib. 2 Fact. 3 Fact. 4 Fib. 5 Fact. 6 Fact. 7 Fact. 8 Fib. 9 Fib. 10 Fib.

Page 14
Where are the Birdies?
3 Tikis
1 Prof. Purplex
2 Peppys
3 DJ Quacks

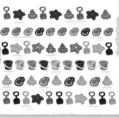

Page 15
Batty Cap'n Buck!
The odd blurp out is 3.
The odd Cap'n Buck out is D.